HAUS CURIOSITIES

Greed

About the Author

Stewart Sutherland is one of Britain's most distinguished philosophers of religion, the author of *Faith and Ambiguity* and *God, Jesus and Belief: The Legacy of Theism*. A cross-bench peer since 2001, with special interests in education, care needs and research, Sutherland served as Vice Chancellor of the Universities of Edinburgh and London, as Principal of King's College London, and as Her Majesty's Chief Inspector of Schools.

Stewart Sutherland

GREED

From Gordon Gekko to David Hume

HAUS
CURIOSITIES

First published by Haus Publishing in 2014
70 Cadogan Place
London SW1X 9AH
www.hauspublishing.com

Copyright © Stewart Sutherland, 2014

The right of the author to be identified as the
author of this work has been asserted in accordance
with the Copyright, Designs and Patents Act 1988

A CIP catalogue record for this book
is available from the British Library

Print ISBN: 978-1-908323-79-8
Ebook ISBN: 978-1-908323-80-4

Typeset in Garamond by MacGuru Ltd
info@macguru.org.uk

Printed in Spain

Contents

The problem

'Greed is good'

Gordon Gekko, Wall Street (1984)

'This avidity alone...is...directly destructive of society'

David Hume, A Treatise on Human Nature
(1739–40)

This essay explores the clash of culture and civility between the recent financial failings of our own society and the forewarnings of one of the greatest European thinkers of the eighteenth century. Oliver Stone's film *Wall Street* introduced us to Gordon Gekko, for some the energising, but ultimately for most the obnoxious symbol of a finance-driven economy. In him is writ large the unrestrained excesses of a greed-driven form of capitalism. In contrast, the elegant prose of the eighteenth-century thinker, David Hume, dissects and accentuates the dangers of this direction of travel. With his friend and philosophical innovator, Adam Smith, often seen as one of the founding saints of modern capitalism, Hume was in his own way as lacerating in his criticism of the misapplication of the dogmas of modern money-men as he was about the faults of institutional religion. Unconstrained greed is the heresy of our times. Hume argues that capitalism need not follow its siren calls.

To voice a Humean view of greed even a decade ago, would have been seen as a sign of envy, or prissiness, or left-wing bias. For was not Gekko more on message about what made capitalism tick? Perhaps, rather Gekko had identified the modern version of what Hume's friend Adam Smith had seen as the essential 'hidden hand' which drive economies to grow and expand. However, perhaps not, on two accounts: the first, that this is not an adequate understanding of Adam Smith; the second, that Gekko's picture of greed is more than an extravagant and eccentric characterisation of something which is fairly humdrum. For after all is it not fairly predictable that those in a position to do so will keep the twenty-pound note found on the footpath, buy shares that are comparatively cheap in the hope that they will rise in value, or seek the best interest rates for their modest savings?

What is the evidence for the presence of even a moderately Gekko-style greed in our society? One does not have to accept the details of Thomas Picketty's analysis of modern capitalism to ask questions about the impact of, for example, information technology on the generation of capital value and profits. The financial and banking collapse and its causes in, as well as its influence on, individual human behaviour that although not predicted by the pundits, has shown a side of modern life which has an obvious resonance with Hume's comment about 'the destructive nature' of avidity. It would be too simplistic to see a human motivation, greed, as simple cause of the post-2008 perturbations and near financial collapse. However, a return to business as usual is, as I shall argue, myopic. The shape of the incentives, rewards and even forms of admiration which are dominant in our society have a profound influence on human behaviour.

One significant change, as I have already mentioned, is that it is no longer bad form or bad taste to use the word 'greed' before the nine o'clock watershed. In the polite company of, for example, *The Times* or the *Sunday Times'* Business section, we may once again use the word and ask questions about its application. There is a perception shared with Hume that greed is not culture-bound, it is an element of the human condition:

'....cupidity is a human characteristic...'
(*Times* Editorial, 27 October 2012)

And its sister paper, the *Sunday Times*, included this header in its Business Section of 16 February 2014: 'Fear and greed are driving a stampede of companies to the stock market.'

Even more significantly, regular comment pieces and news reports in the financial pages make implicit and explicit connections between dubious human motives and accepted financial practices. These stretch from the scandals over fixing Libor or foreign exchange rates to maximise personal and corporate profit, to the ingenious and sometimes crass attempts to circumnavigate regulation on bonuses.

For example:

'HSBC's stars to bypass bonus crackdown' (*The Times*, Business headline 25 February 2014).

And, for variety:

'"Grand in your hand" bonuses cost Lloyds Bank dearly...' (*The Times*, 12 December 2013).

The latter article charts the weird and not so wonderful ways in which the Halifax staff bonus scheme skewed 'a high proportion of sales' to 'potentially unsuitable' customer outcomes. A *Sunday Times* Business headline a few days later referred to this as part of 'a toxic culture'. Even more shocking is *The Times'* Business headline of the previous day, 'Insurer's fine for preying on the elderly'. And so one could go on. Even discounting the natural penchant of many journalists for a striking phrase, this limited sample of what is now fairly commonplace in the responsible press should alert us to a problem.

There are two points here, both of which, as we shall see, endorse Hume's extreme conclusion that avidity is the most destructive of the vices. The first is that greed is a universal characteristic of individual human beings. The second is that it can be encouraged or moderated by the shape which we give to our society. In fact, even more critical than the latter is Hume's view that if it is not restrained, then the consequence could well be the total collapse of the society in which we live.

This is clearly quite the contrary to Gekko's view that the life-blood of commerce, and therefore society, depends upon recognising that 'greed is good'. Some have wanted to enlist Hume's friend Adam Smith on the side of the hardline money-men who insist that making profit and expanding the economy is in fact enlightened self-interest, and that this is a duty and indeed even a virtue. This is a mistaken reading of Adam Smith. But more of that anon. The next section of this pamphlet will analyse the reasons which Hume gave for his harsh judgement on avidity.

David Hume: destructive
or creative sceptic?

Hume's account of the nature of avidity is one very specific and pointed example of his analysis of the nature of society. The starting point for this is the outcome of his agonised and healing years as a young man in France, the first two books of his *Treatise of Human Nature* (1739–40). This revolutionary work, famously, in Hume's own words, 'fell stillborn from the press'. Yet this was the calm before the storm.

As the main early themes reached a wider audience and impact, Hume became a marked man. The chief characterisation, in an age of conventional faith, was as a 'sceptic', and this persists to this day. It is not unfair, but we tend to forget that to be a sceptic is not necessarily to be a cynic or a nihilist. There was more to his philosophy than that. However, given his use of wit and irony – red hot spikes to the sensitivities of the 'unco guid' (or the Religiously Righteous) of his day – and the sharpness of those intellectual tools, it is hardly surprising that he fell foul of much of the establishment. He was for example denied professorships in Philosophy at both his alma mater, the University of Edinburgh, and its sister University of Glasgow. Yet at least in hindsight we see him as probably the most important philosopher to have lived and worked in these islands.

It was not simply that, for example, his philosophy undermined the authority of the Church, it was a matter of the intellectual penetration of his sceptical darts. He concluded his discussion of miracles in his *Enquiry Concerning Human Understanding* thus:

'So that, upon the whole, we may conclude, that the Christian Religion was not only at first attended with miracles, but even at this day cannot be believed by any reasonable person without one'.[1] And of course he was not easily forgiven for referring constantly to religion as superstition. (See for example his Essay 'Of Superstition'.)

On the subject of morality, he was even more pointed and explicit:

"'Tis not contrary to reason to prefer the destruction of the whole world to the scratching of my finger.'[2] Invoking the spectre of Caligula here is comparable to making the point today by arguing that whatever they were, the excesses of a Stalin or a Hitler, were not mistakes in their reasoning power, or in their capacity to draw a syllogistic conclusion from an accepted premise. Thus in addition to rejecting religion as the source of moral distinctions, he was equally decisive in his rejection of rationalism, or appeal to the use of reason alone. And, despite the fact that he was central to the development of what came to be known as 'Scottish Common Sense Philosophy', he did not resort to appeal to some form of innate sense as the source of moral distinctions: 'In general, it may be affirmed, that there is no passion in human minds, as the love of mankind merely as such, independent of personal qualities, of services, or of relation to ourself'.[3]

We must note, however, that the consequent tendency to dismiss Hume as the master of negativity is equally far from the mark. This shows in general in two ways. The first is that he was also explicit in his insistence that his comments on scratching fingers did not mean that he dismissed the significance of moral approbation and disapprobation: 'Morality is a subject that interests us above all others: We fancy the peace of society to be at stake in every decision concerning it'.[4] This came at the outset of the third Book of his *Treatise*, published a year after the first two Books. For good measure, as Hume re-emphasised at the outset of his *Enquiry Concerning the Principles of Morals*, 'Those who have denied the reality of moral distinctions must be ranked among the disingenuous disputants'.[5]

This, however, emphasises the legitimacy of the question put over the years to Hume: What alternative account can you give about the nature of moral distinctions, and about the bonds which hold society together? Or are you simply a sceptic with no positive philosophy?

Hume has answers to these questions, but it has to be accepted that these are not spelt out as systematically as the case for scepticism in the *Treatise* Book I. This is therefore the point to give a health warning. What follows is a systematization of what we find in Hume – in Book III of the *Treatise* and in his Essays and to some extent his historical works. Distinctions will be drawn which were more fashionable in the twentieth century than in the eighteenth, but these are simply means to grasp what is of lasting significance in Hume's analysis of the nature of society.

The second defence of Hume against the charge of negativity is now the central focus of our exposition: Hume's own account of the role of justice and equity in the conditions necessary for the maintenance of civil society.

Self-assertion or 'sympathy'?

Hume's intentions and aspirations are writ large on the title page of his first great revolutionary work: 'A Treatise of Human Nature: Being An Attempt to introduce the experimental Method of Reasoning into Moral Subjects'. The fundamental principle of his work was a commitment to empiricism. In this he followed the philosopher John Locke, but beyond that the dominant intellectual influence of the day was to be found in the work of Isaac Newton. Philosophers and others were entranced by the reshaping of our understanding of the physical world which Newton had forged through the reflection upon evidence and fact.

In conjunction with a number of others, for example Adam Ferguson and Adam Smith, Hume early grasped that the methods of physical science could be applied to human society as well as to individual human beings. Ferguson's *Essay on the History of Civil Society* (1767)[6] is arguably the first systematic attempt to understand the nature of human society in self-consciously empirical terms, and of course the impact of Adam Smith's *The Wealth of Nations* (1776) is difficult to overestimate. Hume's first systematic contribution to such an empirical understanding of human society, the *Treatise*, predates both of these, and was complemented by his historical writings. (He shared much with Smith, including a sense of the importance of the study of history.)

Greed and Self

Basically, Hume believed that we are as individuals self-centred. In moderation of this rather gloomy view Hume also believed that we had the capacity to develop what he was reluctant to call a moral sense, but which was a capacity to respond to human action, our own and others', with moral approval or disapproval. The development of this capacity was part of the establishment of human relations and human society, although our natural dispositions were self-centred.

Our love, or admiration, or even distaste for others is specific to individuals and is moderated by our distance from or proximity to them in space, time and other relationships. It is not simply an application of some generalised 'love of mankind'. We are in that sense, naturally 'selfish', or self-centred in the sense of focussed within our own concentric spheres of association in our appraisal of others. That appraisal, admiration, distrust or whatever, depends initially and naturally on the relationship we have to those others. Offspring, parents, siblings, are closer than more distant relatives or friends, and so do the eddies of sentiment spread outwards less vigorously to inhabitants of the same locality or city or nation. Naturally, Hume suggests, the closer the link, the greater the likelihood of positive or, we might add 'distorted' sentiments and emotions. This is seen at its most extreme in the earliest days of childhood where the needs and demands of self predominate in relationships to others. And when this is allied to the growing skills of emotional manipulation, many parents experience the impact of emergent self-assertion red in tooth and claw – 'the terrible twos'.* How then are the constraints of self-discipline given place over the natural energies of self-assertion and self-gratification?

The clues in Hume's writings point in the following direction.

In the first place within the family, the little bundle of demand and self-assertion

---

*It is in part this seemingly unrelenting assessment of human nature which led some philosophers, most notably Norman Kemp Smith, in his introduction to Hume's *Dialogues Concerning Natural Religion* (2nd Ed. Edinburgh, 1947), to stress Hume's Calvinist background. The difference from some preachers of his day is that his lack of high sentiment did not lead him to universal damnation of his fellow men and women. Rather this is what provoked his search for a science of human nature which would attend to the facts, that notwithstanding the above, civil society is possible.

that is a child develops an awareness that others have needs and demands: the others initially are those closest to us, on whom we depend and with whom the benefits of positive relationships are most obvious.

In the second place, although his reservations include the possibility that 'education' could be used for all sorts of indoctrination, education played an essential part in human development, not least in emotional and moral development. Nowhere is this more the case than in giving us a perspective on others, which he associated with the development of what he called 'sympathy'. This latter was at the heart of his account of moral approbation which requires another and longer discussion (see for example Philip Mercer's *Sympathy and Ethics*[7]). It was shared with and further refined by Adam Smith, and is probably better more nearly characterised by the modern term 'empathy'.

The third mechanism which helped, or even required enhanced awareness of sharing with others is the power of language and communication.

Engagement through each of these with the world beyond self-interest, family, education into the ways of 'sympathy', and the sharing of a language was for Hume the developmental road to engagement in society. Licensing, let alone canonising, greed is regressive to all of that – regressive to the point of containing the seeds of destruction.

This is the first pillar of Hume's claim that avidity is the most destructive of the vices. The looser the social constraints on greed the greater the loosening of the essential ties which lead from primitive self-assertion to civilised engagement in society. Unlicensed greed is the absence of all that Hume builds into the civilising process of belonging to society. Such greed is the rejection of all that builds moral sensibility, for it is the re-assertion of self over the recognition of the reasonable demands and needs of others, and of the limits which this

should set to self-assertion. Hume is imply-
ing that the guiding bonds of engagement
in family, education and language are processes which in fact work. Those who disa-
gree with him are invited to give adequate
empirical grounds for other proposed civilising processes.

The second critical pillar is Hume's
account of the role of justice and equity* in
sustaining and enhancing the stability of
society. Indeed he would go further than that
for the protection of justice and equity were
not simply the advantages which society
could confer on its members. There comes a
point where justice and equity are constitu-
tive of what civil society is, and their absence
is destructive rather than merely regretful
or demeaning. In this Hume's friend Adam
Smith offered support both in his *Theory*

---

*Equity is not the same as equality, but has to
do with a rather more fluid account of what is
pragmatically acceptable in society. This is why it
is so much a matter of contention and debate, but
more of that anon.

of Moral Sentiments and his seminal *The Wealth of Nations.*

Stability, Property and Greed

'Without justice, society must
immediately dissolve.'[8]

'Property must be stable and must be
fixed by general rules.'[9]

David Hume, *A Treatise of Human Nature*

These in addition to protecting the citizens
are the key roles of society:

1. to establish the theory and practice
   of justice, and
2. to establish the general and
   universally applicable rules of
   ownership and property.

This latter is an essential condition of the
functioning and sustainability of society.
Owning something applies as much to a

hammer as a house, a barrow as a bungalow. If we sell a car, there must be legal ownership in the first place, which is then transferred by agreed processes to the purchaser. If we have title to a piece of ground – allotment or estate – we must be able to justify the claim or prove that this is so, according to custom and law. The very idea of a credit card or a mobile telephone being stolen implies legitimate ownership being replaced through the practice of stealth, violence or cunning, by illegal possession.

The stability of property is part of the structure of society, not a consequence of the 'creation' of society. Hume was offering an account of the conditions necessary for the existence and sustainability of civil society, not a description of how society had evolved. Society was not, in his view, created to protect property; outside society property (with all that implies about legality and process) does not exist. Outside of society we may merely possess things and defend the possession of those things by violence, cunning and theft.

The extreme example of the awareness of this was the temporary introduction of the death penalty for looting in the early part of the Second World War. This was publicly reasserted immediately following the catastrophic bombing of Coventry in 1940.

'Without the stability of property, society must immediately dissolve' the ghost of Hume whispered into Churchill's ear. And even more so in time of war this applies to the remnants of property remaining after the destruction of the Blitz. The rise of the practice of war on civilian populations is the expression of the realisation that the destruction of society rather than simply the defeat of the nation is possible. Society is nowhere more vulnerable than by attack on the rules of justice, equity and ownership. Such collapse of the norms, rights and expectations of society is what happens when the rule of law breaks down.

In times such as these, or even in less dramatic moments, theft as much as looting stretches the sinews of tolerance in a hitherto stable society. Stealth and cunning replace violence as the mechanism, but there are limits to the mutual tolerance made possible by equitable and just rules and processes of ownership. Now of course this is not a plea for the utopian picture of society free of theft and cunning. But it is a warning of the dangers of the unconstrained exercise of either. Gekko recommends a high-octane, rewards-version of the latter in his guiding principle, 'Greed is good'. Hume acknowledges the human tendency upon which Gekko is leaning, but sees beyond Gekko and his supreme mastery of the stealth and cunning which he practises: after warning us that the uninhibited expression of basic human nature is incompatible with what he calls 'the association of individuals' as 'society', he continues: 'that association never could have place were no regard paid to the laws of equity and justice. Disorder, confusion, the war of all against all are the necessary consequence of such conduct'. A much quoted line from *The Theory of Moral*

Sentiments shows how close Hume and Adam Smith were on this: 'Justice ... is the pillar that upholds the whole edifice. If it is removed, the great, the immense fabric of human society ... must in a moment crumble into atoms.'[10] At the heart of this Hume sees a central conclusion of his attempt to introduce empirical procedures to the study of human nature: 'This avidity alone of acquiring goods and possessions for ourselves and our nearest friends, is insatiable, universal and directly destructive of society'.[11]

Duncan Forbes, in his excellent, *Hume's Philosophical Politics*, glosses and refines this further: 'We expect men to be unjust, because it is in order to get security against this that government is established: we change the situation, but not the nature of men who are to be our magistrates, making it their immediate interest to rule justly'.[12] This underlines a point made earlier that 'greed' or 'avidity' or 'cupidity', are human characteristics, but that there are limits to how far keeping these in check is a matter solely of individual character and psychology. Containing these is in part a necessary condition of the continuation of society, and is also possible only within the structures of a well-ordered society. The problem is what I have earlier called 'systemic'.

To summarise, Hume's view is that greed unconstrained is destructive of society. Part of the reason for this is that it is not bound by rules of justice, equity and ownership. If the race seems to be to the strong, then in this context, strength is the exercise of cunning, intelligence and unscrupulousness in the pursuit of power and possession for oneself and one's nearest and dearest. Of course, greed can be practised within the law, and sometimes on the fringes of the law. Hume is however concerned to point out the extreme consequences of unrestrained greed. Hume's insight is that greed minimises the claims of others, and absolute greed minimises absolutely the claims of others. It minimises absolutely the notion of justice and equity for other human beings, and minimises absolutely the possibility of possession of property on other grounds than the capacity of the owner to wrest it from others through the practices of stealth, cunning and violence.

Greed and Inequity

If this analysis is anywhere near the truth of the matter, then what are the consequences for the Gordon Gekkos of this world? The first point to make is that any such individual that we know about is a paler imitation (the Gekko-lite versions). If there are real living Gekkos out there, then we probably don't know about them, we are simply subject to the consequences of their successful and absolute practice of their motto 'greed is good'.

However, that there are plenty of apprentice and even journeyman Gekkos has become more and more apparent as various scandals have been uncovered. One group of these have involved illegal activities, and prosecutions have been varyingly successful. They have involved, for example, breaking rules of banking practice, some apparently trying to 'fix' Libor and exchange rates. According to recent reports, the Serious Fraud Office is already this on particular trail. To take one headline from the *Sunday Times* Business section: 'Banks on rack as SFO launches probe into currency trading' (20 July 2014).

Some of course have been probing attempts to test the limits of regulation and legality, very often in the uncertain eddies which flow between tax evasion and tax avoidance. Others, however, have been questions of proportion and reward, and of our understanding of what equity is in our society. Is an annual reward of £27 million at all within the bounds of this elastic concept of equity, not least if it is compared with the lowest-earning members on the payroll of the same company?

These latter examples raise many questions critical for the nature, and Hume would argue, sustainability of the society which we inhabit. We are already immersed in the questions of when a tax avoidance scheme which is technically legal is 'unacceptable' – is it simply when HMRC, or the Chancellor of the Exchequer, or the leader of the Labour Party, or the *Daily Mirror* or the *Guardian* says so?

Two issues predominate here and should preoccupy us: the first is how do we define 'inequity' or 'injustice', or set the rules for 'ownership'; the second is how do we regulate or influence such principles. Hume can help us with both of these questions, but his first and major point is that they are not trivial: '...were no regard paid to the laws of equity and justice...disorder, confusion, the war of all against all are the necessary consequences.' 'Without justice,' he continues 'society must immediately dissolve.'[13]

Hume is clear then, that to call greed the most destructive of the vices is neither metaphor nor hyperbole. If greed runs unlicensed, unconstrained then the sinews of society can be drawn taut to breaking point. The fundamental reason is that society is the civilising of the individual, and of the individual's natural direction of travel. Society is the recognition and instantiation of the capacity to approve in others what does not necessarily directly serve our own self-interest. Society is the context within which we can accept, and act on, the disapproval of an action that might promote the satisfaction of our own immediate demands. Society rests in part on the capacity to take pride in our promotion of the interests of others, and shame in the wilful thwarting of those.

Against that picture, the practice of greed is not merely *not* good, it is positively destructive. That, Hume believes, is what the empirical procedures of his embryonic 'science of human nature' tell us.

So What?

In this concluding section we may speculate about what this proposes about how to deal with the universal human characteristic of greed. These proposals fall into two different categories. The first is at the individual level, the second at the structural and public level.

The Individual

Hume makes plain the process of civilising what Shakespeare characterises as the 'mewling and puking' age. This has three strands to it.

Strand 1: The family

The first is the experience of the family, and the gradual process of tempering the demands of the self with the competing demands of siblings, parents and in general those who surround the child. This will seem to some terribly old-fashioned, terribly conventional, but the challenge is to suggest an alternative route. Perhaps the notion of the kibbutz has possibilities and sadly for some, alternative forms of 'looked-after' life have had to be developed. On the latter all the evidence suggests that the often heroic attempts to make this work – especially beyond the quasi-family of the foster home – are second and often third best. Nonetheless they are the best options which we have so far developed. The Humean point is that at least to attempt to find a substitute in the absence of the natural family, is to start in the right direction.

I have no empirical basis for commenting on the success or otherwise of the kibbutz movement, other than that my Jewish friends who have emigrated to Israel have done so to enhance family life rather than to replace it with an alternative.

Strand 2: Language

Hume's second point is that as a matter of fact, the very process of learning to inhabit a language is a process of inclusion within a society. We learn that the processes of defining meaning and clarity are independent of the purely self-focussed grunts, growls and snarls of immaturity, although the latter and their transcendence is the route towards the civilising structures of communication. There is no doubt that handicap in this area inhibits human flourishing.

Strand 3: Education

Hume had mixed views of education, for he was well aware that it could be misused as well as used – certainly in formal contexts. However, he was not in doubt that education, formal and informal, was an indispensable pillar of the shaping of society and the individuals who constitute that society. The development of what he referred to by the technical term 'sympathy' depends upon the use of empirical and non-empirical reasoning as well as the enhancement of the imagination.

This is not the point to begin an exposition of the nature of good educational practice, but it should be clear that in formal contexts this is the major contribution which society makes to the process of 'civilising'. (One point of empirical evidence is the appallingly low educational attainments of those who find themselves temporarily off of the main highway of society – in prison. The statistics of illiteracy and lack of basic numerical skills are neon-lit warnings.)

Of course, an even greater part of education of the young takes place outside the formal structures of the classroom – through parents, friends (and enemies), the surrounding culture, and increasingly today through self-controlled technology. (We have gone beyond the offerings of radio, of television, to the tablet and the smart phone. In a Humean world we are urged to respond to the possibilities as well as pitfalls of this as a civilising encounter.)

In education one of the key messages is to re-think the place of the education of the emotions in formal as well as informal settings. What are the differences between the emotions surrounding shame and inadequacy? In Hume's world the concepts of shame and indeed pride have a place in the emotional range of a money-man or a banker. In Gekko's world the only bad banker is an inadequate one. Learning these distinctions which constitute part of the moral awareness on which society is built, is in part a task for education, formal and informal.

The constraints of society

The type of society we inhabit is formative of much of who we are and what we do. At the core of this, according to Hume, are the concepts of justice and equity. Not so for Gekko. Justice, he might think, like lunch, is for wimps.

In the context of greed, justice has to do with the fair and equitable application of law to every citizen. This is a matter of practicality as well as high principle. It requires structures and infrastructures. Particularly, Hume emphasises, this relates to the laws defining property and legitimate ownership. These require the structures necessary to authenticate and defend that ownership.

Greed tells us that it is more a matter of smartness with a tendency to cunning to establish or change ownership – why else, in an adversarial system is there a such a dramatic correlation between between the skills of a lawyer or accountant and the price of his or her services? The skilful accountant or adversarial lawyer is paid more because there is more money at stake, and greed becomes ever more insistent. This is a good indicator of the tendency to a hierarchy of values in our society. Of course, this correlation may well help encapsulate the principle that reward should be proportionate to skills, but it militates against the equally important principle that the justice of court decisions should be available to all and not just to those who can afford the best legal mercenaries.

I am by no means naive enough to assume that there are simple solutions here, but justice should not be threatened by the depths of corporate or individual pockets. The latter is an empowerment of the 'greed is good' slogan. Equally since many of the related public issues here have to do with corporate and individual practice – which is, in Aristotle's term a 'techne' or a skill, rather than a matter of simply distinguishing the legal from the illegal – there are two important mechanisms here.

The first, and easiest to identify, is the mechanism of formal regulation of professional practice. This has become increasingly well developed in our society, but it has two potential weaknesses: the first is inadequacy, and there has been recent evidence of that in the financial world. Regulators need clear remits, independent advice and the powers to engage with very sophisticated organisations and practices. This is a primary role of the state. But, easier said than consistently done, it must not constrain legitimate originality and enterprise.

This shows the need for a second and more informal mechanism of controlling greed. This is the willingness to refocus in our society the role of concepts such as shame, especially when related to proportionality. Very few in our society would insist that total equality in the distribution of the benefits of society is a sensible or positive aim. Human beings need not to be the champions of greed to see the advantages of profit, or of differentiated pay and rewards. Many of us appreciate the benefits of tax relief for specific reasons – charitable giving, inheritance of wife from husband and vice-versa. An ISA here or there, on the whole, seems a legitimate aspiration. And so on. The difficulties for society arise, albeit initially informally, when rewards seem disproportionate, or tax relief schemes shimmy towards tax-avoidance – as they undoubtedly do in some cases.

Here, there may be a role for more informal mechanisms – some already in play. What is now known by the catchy title of 'naming and shaming' has its dangers and can thrive on a witch-hunt mentality: however, it also has its power to satisfy reasonable instincts for equity and proportionality. It is one thing to be rewarded for brilliant invention or market sensitivity, quite another to enhance the benefit through what seem to be at best rather dodgy tax schemes in far distant places or corners of the fiscal practice.

I have a rather blunt instrument to propose here, but before turning to that doubtless outrageous suggestion, let us reflect for a further moment on the role of public awareness and discussion.

This is most critical at times of upheaval and disruption. Most of the time those of us who are not the significant beneficiaries are aware that the accumulation of wealth is a vibrant strand of our society. We accept that there is probably 'trickle-down', and that as Adam Smith argued cogently, all of this adds to the common good, because it is still possible to talk of the wealth of the nation as well as the wealth of individuals and dynasties.

However, from time to time the even tenor of society's economic development is severely disrupted and 'certainties' fail us. It is then that the disruption opens up chasms of doubt, possibly, fear and certainly envy. Hume's worry is that these chasms might become destructive of society. These events may have been shaped in some corners by greed, and certainly they expose examples of the 'greed is good' mantra.

This is the point at which it is essential to open up a public discussion of what justice and equity is in these matters. There may be appropriate rules, as suggested by some on a European-wide basis on limiting annual bonuses. But if greed is still the driving force, then we will have headlines very soon about clever schemes to avoid the rules. There may be conventions developed about the ratio of top salaries in any company and the rewards offered to the lowest-paid employees, but it is unlikely that a simple single multiplier will be the best ultimate solution in all contexts. There may be changes to inheritance tax, but there will be arguments to be heard on both sides.

My own rather shocking starting point would be the oxygen of publicity. Perhaps making all tax returns, individual and corporate, a matter of public record – possibly within two, three, five or even ten years of submission – would be a good starting point. There is no doubt that public awareness of the tax contribution which the Amazons of this world make to this country is a good starting point for a discussion of proportionality. Equally the more sensitive area of publicly-available information about the individual contribution made by some to the tax revenues of the nation would in some cases dispel myths, but in others raise fundamental questions of equity. After all even the Queen is subject to significant intrusion here!

But to conclude with a final health warning: this suggestion comes from your

author rather than from Hume! It is Hume
that gives the more important advice: greed
is 'the most destructive of the vices'.

Notes

1. David Hume, *An Enquiry Concerning Human Understanding and an Enquiry Concerning the Principles of Morals*, quoted in ed. L.A. Selby-Bigge (1894, Clarendon Press) p.131.

2. David Hume, *A Treatise of Human Nature*, 1739–40, quoted in ed. L.A. Selby-Bigge (1896, Clarendon Press) p.416.

3. Hume, *A Treatise of Human Nature*, p.481.

4. Hume, *A Treatise of Human Nature*, p.456.

5. Hume, *An Enquiry Concerning the Principles of Morals*, p.169.

6. Ferguson's *Essay on the History of Civil Society* is most conveniently referenced in ed. Duncan Forbes (Edinburgh, 1966).

7. Philip Mercer, *Sympathy and Ethics* (Oxford University Press, 1966).

8. Hume, *A Treatise of Human Nature*, p.497.

9. Hume, *A Treatise of Human Nature*, p.497.

10. D.D. Raphael and J.L. Mackie II. iii. 3.4.

11. *A Treatise of Human Nature*, pp.491–2.

12. Duncan Forbes, *Hume's Philosophical Politics* (Cambridge University Press, 1985) pp.12–13.

13. *A Treatise of Human Nature*, p.497.